HISTORY IN ART

ANCIENT GREECE

Chicago, Illinois

ANDREW LANGLEY

Originated by Dot Gradations.
Printed and bound in China,
by South China Printing Company.

09 08 07 06
10 9 8 7 6 5 4 3 2

Library of Congress Cataloging-in-Publication Data

Langley, Andrew.
  Ancient Greece / Andrew Langley.
     p. cm. -- (History in art)
  ISBN 1-4109-0517-9
  1. Art, Greek--Juvenile literature. 2. Greece--Civilization--To 146 B.C.--Juvenile literature. I. Title. II. Series.
  N5633.L28 2005
  709'.38--dc22

                                        2004007523

Acknowledgments
The publishers would like to thank the following for permission to reproduce photographs (t) = top (b) = bottom): AKG pp. **8**, **9** (Erich Lessing), **12** (Cameraphoto), **15**(b) (John Hios), **23**(t) (John Hios), **24**(t), **38**(t) (Erich Lessing); Ancient Art and Architecture pp. **10** (Brian Gibbs), **16** (B. Norman), **30**(t & b) (Ronald Sheridan); Bridgeman Art Library pp. **4**(t), **5**, **6**, **7**(b), **11**, **13**, **14**, **15**(t) (Lauros/ Giraudon), **20** (Alinari), **21**(t) (Peter Willi), **21**(b), **22** (Peter Willi), **25**, **24**(b) (Giraudon), **25**(b) (Giraudon), **26**, **27** (Bonhams, London, UK), **28**, **29**(t), **29**(b) (Peter Willi), **31**, **32**, **33**(t & b), **34**, **35**(b) (Bildarchiv Steffens), **36** (Lauros/Giraudon), **37**(t), **37**(b) (Lauros/ Giraudon), **38**(b) (Peter Willi), **39** (Bildarchiv Steffens), **40**, **41**, **42** (Alinari); Harcourt/Corbis **17**(t); Harcourt Education Ltd. **18**; Museum of Fine Arts, Houston, Texas, USA/www.bridgeman.co.uk pp. **43**; The Art Archive pp. **19** (Museo Nazionale Terme Rome/ Dagli Orti), **23**(b) (Museo Nazionale Taranto/Dagli Orti), **35**(t) (National Archaeological Museum Athens/Dagli Orti); The Detroit Institute of Arts, USA/www.bridgeman.co.uk pp. **7**(t); WTPix pp. **4**(b), **17**(b).

Cover photograph of Agamemnon's gold death mask from the second half of the 16th century B.C.E., reproduced with permission of AKG.

Every effort has been made to contact copyright holders of any material reproduced in this book. Any omissions will be rectified in subsequent printings if notice is given to the publishers.

The publisher would like to thank Dr Christina Haywood, Curator of the Classical Museum, University College Dublin, for her assistance in the preparation of this book.

The paper used to print this book comes from sustainable resources.

Contents

Chapter 1 Art as Evidence   4
Learning the Secrets   6

Chapter 2 The Story of Ancient Greece   8
The Birth of the City-state   10
Invasions and Civil War   12
Marching to India   14
Feature: Architecture   16

Chapter 3 Inside the City-state   18
Trade and Warfare   20
Feature: A World of Color   22
Visionaries and Thinkers   24

Chapter 4 Everyday Life   26
Feature: Vase Painting   28
Playing Games   30
Eating and Drinking   32
Theater and the Olympic Games   34

Chapter 5 Religion and Mythology   36
Festivals and Oracles   38
Heroes and Heroines   40
Feature: Marble and Bronze   42

Time line   44
Glossary   46
More Books to Read   47
Index   48

Art as Evidence

"Future generations will marvel at us," predicted Pericles, leader of Athens in about 440 B.C.E., "as the present age marvels at us now." The Greeks themselves knew they were something special. It is indeed amazing that 2,000 years after the decline of the Greek **civilization**, its powerful influence can still be seen in modern **politics** and ideas, art and architecture, and sports and theater.

How do we know about such an ancient civilization? What is left behind to tell us about this long-gone age? **Archaeologists** have found the ruins of many great buildings, as well as thousands of paintings, sculptures, pots, and other remains of the ancient Greek world. The writings of Greek historians, politicians, poets, and playwrights survive, but the biggest and most varied record lies in the work of the artists—certainly some

of the most outstanding ever created. Their marble statues, painted pottery, and massive temples still inspire artists today and provide superb source material about the history, **mythology**, and daily life of ancient Greece.

Greek inspiration

Greek art is all around us. Throughout history, artists of all kinds have used the methods, subjects and inspiration of the ancient Greeks in their work. **Renaissance** sculptors such as Michelangelo were deeply influenced by Greek models. The head of Michelangelo's statue of David (right), completed in 1504, was inspired by the Greeks.

▼ The Acropolis ("stronghold on a hill"), topped by the Parthenon, dominates the skyline of modern Athens. It is one of the most famous historic sites in the world.

Steep rock sides of the Acropolis

Fortified walls at the top

The Erechtheum

The Parthenon

Pictures of the past

The pictures on vases and other pottery show in wonderful detail what the Greeks ate and wore, and how they entertained themselves, as well as countless episodes from their myths. Mythical adventures and important moments in Greek history are illustrated in carvings and wall paintings. The many nude male statues produced help us to recognize the Greeks' reverence for the human body. Great buildings, such as the Parthenon in Athens and the theater at Epidaurus, tell us a huge amount about Greek religion and public life. All the same, this treasury of source material must be treated with caution. It would be wrong solely to rely on **artifacts** like these to give us a complete and realistic picture of Greek life. Vivid though they are, the pictures and statues tell us only part of the story. Greek sculptors wanted to portray human beauty in their work, but this does not mean that all Greek youths were beautiful!

We have to interpret what we see and look beyond the surface, because these works of art also give us less obvious information. By studying them, we can find out how they were made, who made them, and what materials were used. This provides us with evidence of what sort of technology was available to the Greeks—for **casting bronze** statues, turning clay vases, or transporting and lifting big blocks of marble.

The goddess Nike (Victory) carries a garland.

◀ The winged Nike, Greek symbol of victory in battle, is shown in flight in this delicate vase painting from about 430 B.C.E.

Bronze tripod, with legs fixed to stone base.

*The stone **column** supports the bowl for sacrificial offerings.*

Gold patterns at the top and bottom act as frames for the picture.

5

Learning the Secrets

The art treasures of ancient Greece come in many different shapes and sizes. There are vast temples and tiny carved gemstones, painted vases, and marble statues. All of these things give us not only a lot of pleasure but also vital clues about Greek life and manners, if we look at them properly. Before studying this rich source material, we have to decide how informative it may be by answering some questions.

Who made these **artifacts**? We know the names of some of the artists. A few vase painters put signatures on their work ("Exekias painted me," reads one vase), but most of the rest are unknown and probably saw themselves as merely craftworkers rather than artists.

There were, however, many sculptors, such as Praxiteles, and wall painters, such as Zeuxis. who were celebrities throughout Greece.

Who did these artists and craftspeople work for? Only the rich and powerful, including kings and queens, could afford to pay the best sculptors and painters. They bought the most beautifully painted vases and commissioned carved memorial stones for their family graves. By far the biggest employer was the state. Public money was used to pay for the building of enormous temples such as the Parthenon, the great temple in the city of Athens, and to fill them with magnificent statues and wall paintings.

▼ This wall painting shows a procession of warriors from a Greek tomb built in the 300s B.C.E. in Paestum, southern Italy.

Greaves (armor) to protect lower legs

Breastplate to protect upper body

Decorated shield made of bronze and wood

Long spear for thrusting and stabbing rather than throwing

Bronze helmet

Mounted warrior has no stirrups.

Attendant carrying a torch

An Ornate stopper was used to seal oil inside.

Amphora was given as a prize to a victorious athlete.

Examining the evidence

Temples, sculptures, and other objects can tell us about Greek history, **mythology**, and daily life—as long as we know what to look for. This amphora, or two-handled storage jar, shows athletes running a race. It is one of many such jars that were produced to hold the olive oil made from the fruit of the sacred olive grove dedicated to the goddess Athena. The oil-filled jar was presented to winners of the athletic events at the Panathenaic Festival in Athens, held every four years in honor of Athena, the city's patron goddess.

Athletes normally did not wear clothes while competing.

The long stride and high arm action indicate that they are sprinting.

◀ This Panathenaic amphora shows athletes running. On the other side is a picture of Athena, goddess of the city of Athens. The style of the images, painted in black, reveals that the vase was probably made in about 550 B.C.E.

How has Greek art survived?

In the 2,000 years since the ancient Greek **civilization** faded, many works of art have disappeared. They have been smashed or stolen, or have simply crumbled away. The Parthenon suffered huge damage from a Venetian artillery shell in 1687. Yet a vast amount remains, and fresh finds continue to be made. Since the early 1800s, **archaeologists** have excavated ancient sites such as Delphi, Ephesus, and Thebes, rediscovering many masterpieces of pottery, sculpture, and architecture lying hidden in the earth. Other treasures, such as a **bronze** statue of Zeus, have been found lying under the sea. This painting from the palace at Knossos shows an elaborate **ritual** involving a bull and leaping athletes. Nobody knows exactly what the ritual involved.

The Story of Ancient Greece

The country we now know as Greece is made up of the mainland and many islands that are scattered throughout the Aegean and Adriatic seas. Ancient Greece, however, was neither a unified country nor a centrally controlled **empire** like Rome.

Mycenaeans

The first great **civilization** on the mainland did not appear until about 1600 B.C.E. An **immigrant** group of settlers established their power in the south of Greece and built several important towns. We call them the Mycenaeans, after their hilltop stronghold of Mycenae.

Almost nothing was known about these people until the late 1800s, when **archaeologists** began to excavate Mycenae and nearby sites. They found sensational things—royal tombs crammed with gold and other treasures, pottery, fortified walls—some as much as 26 feet (8 meters) thick—and a massive palace. Most famous of all was the Lion Gate at the main entrance to the palace, with its huge **lintel** topped with a triangular **relief** carving of two lions.

▼ The Lion Gate was the magnificent entrance to the fortress of Mycenae. The city walls were so massive that in later years people thought they could only have been built by giants.

Two relief carvings of lionesses are now headless.

The huge stone blocks of the walls are cut to fit precisely together.

The triangular gap around the carvings helps to spread the weight on the enormous lintel stone underneath.

The lintel stone is 15 ft. (4.5 m) long and 6 ft. (2 m) wide

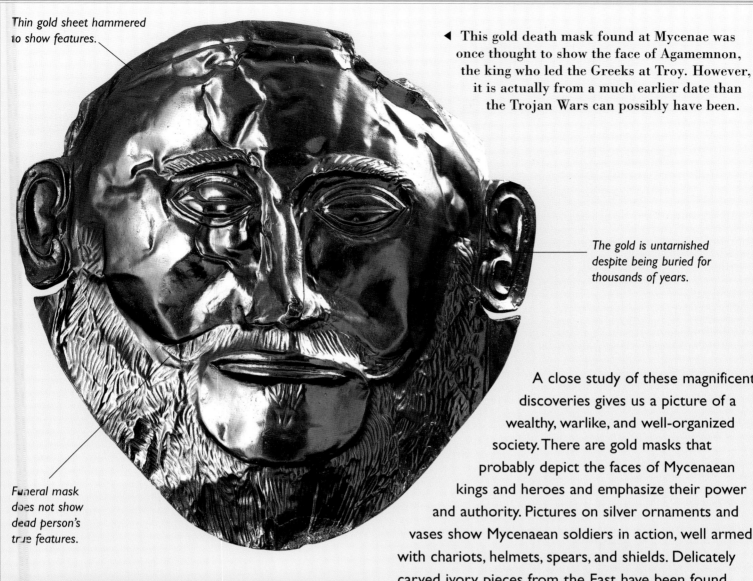

Thin gold sheet hammered to show features.

► This gold death mask found at Mycenae was once thought to show the face of Agamemnon, the king who led the Greeks at Troy. However, it is actually from a much earlier date than the Trojan Wars can possibly have been.

The gold is untarnished despite being buried for thousands of years.

Funeral mask does not show dead person's true features.

A close study of these magnificent discoveries gives us a picture of a wealthy, warlike, and well-organized society. There are gold masks that probably depict the faces of Mycenaean kings and heroes and emphasize their power and authority. Pictures on silver ornaments and vases show Mycenaean soldiers in action, well armed with chariots, helmets, spears, and shields. Delicately carved ivory pieces from the East have been found, telling us that there must have been trading contacts with lands such as Egypt and the Levant (the eastern Mediterranean).

The Trojan War

The **epic** of the Greeks' siege of Troy is one of the best-known stories in the world. It tells of a war lasting nine years, with characters including Achilles, Helen of Troy, Odysseus, and Ajax, as well as gods and goddesses. No one knows for certain if and when the conflict actually took place. Archaeologists have found evidence that a city on the site of Troy, on the coast of **Asia Minor** (or modern Turkey), was destroyed in about 1250 B.C.E. Homer's poem *The Iliad* tells episodes from the siege of Troy, but this was probably written at least 400 years afterward. Whatever the truth of the Trojan Wars, their heroes, heroines, and deeds became a central part of Greek **mythology**, and the key scenes appear in many sculptures and vase paintings.

The Dark Ages and after

By about 1100 B.C.E., the power of the Mycenaeans was gone. The palaces and fortresses were destroyed and the villages abandoned, possibly after a savage civil war. Greece moved into what historians have called the Dark Ages, a period that lasted for more than three centuries. Archaeologists know very little about this period. Some Greeks moved overseas to escape the poverty of their native land.

The Birth of the City-state

Greece is a land of steep mountain ranges, with relatively few areas of flat land that can be farmed between them. Most of the early communities grew up in these valleys, or on the narrow coastal plains, but the mountainous landscapes kept them separate from each other. So it was that these scattered communities developed into city-states with strong individual identities.

Polis

This kind of independent society, with control over an area of country around a fortified center, was called a *polis*. Some were very small in size, but each ran its own affairs, with its own army, parliament, laws, and coinage. Many built their strongholds on hills with steep sides and flat tops. This kind of stronghold was called the *acropolis*, or "high city."

▼ These are ruins of the Temple of Apollo at Corinth, with the city's *acropolis* (the Acrocorinth) behind. Corinth became powerful during the 400s B.C.E. because it controlled the narrow strip of land joining the Peloponnesus to the rest of Greece.

The mountain of the Acrocorinth

Doric **columns** of the Temple of Apollo, once the center of the ancient city

Fortified walls

Surrounded by a thick wall, the *acropolis* was an ideal spot for people to take shelter when attacked by enemies. It was also a center of worship, with the main temples and other important buildings grouped there. The cost, labor, and care put into these structures show the importance of religion in the city-states. Among the best known of these strongholds are the Acropolis in Athens, the Acrocorinth near the city of Corinth, and Lindos on the island of Rhodes.

Power to the people

It is from "*polis*" that we get the modern word "**politics**", or the science of running a state or community. The Greeks developed this science, exploring the meaning of justice and law, and examining new and fairer ways of governing people. Kings and queens disappeared early in Greek history, and power came into the hands of the wealthy **aristocrats**. The poor had no political rights, owned no land, and were virtually slaves for their rich rulers.

▶ This vase has survived intact because it was placed in a grave.

The "key" motif was very popular in Greek art.

Zones of different patterns cover the whole vase.

From about 650 B.C.E., the aristocrats found themselves being pushed aside by the "tyrants" (from the Greek word *tyrannos*), who seized power by force. Many tyrants were actually popular at first. In Corinth, the tyrant threw out the aristocrats, who were hated by the people. In Megara and Samos, the new ruler installed a water supply. It was not long, however, before the tyrants lost the support of the people. As a result, an early form of **democracy**, or rule by the people, began to be introduced, with voting rights for all (wealthy) male citizens. Greece's greatest period was about to begin.

Inspiration from the East

As trade routes grew and overseas settlements were founded, pottery, jewelry, and other fine things were imported into Greece, and the influence of other cultures begins to show in Greek art. Early sculptures of male nudes were closely modeled on statues from Egypt. Vase decorations in the geometric style (see jug, right, made in about 730 B.C.E.) with formal patterns and matchstick figures, gave way to more realistic and detailed pictures of humans and animals, inspired by work from Assyria. This developed into what is known as black-figure painting, with the figures drawn in outlines of black paint.

Invasions and Civil War

During the 400s B.C.E., two wars transformed ancient Greece. At the center of both were the two biggest and most powerful city-states—Athens and Sparta. By 500 B.C.E. Athens and Sparta were growing much faster than the other cities, but in very different ways. Athens, with its new democratic government, was becoming wealthy through overseas trade. Sparta was ruled by two kings, and used its permanent and highly trained army to subdue neighboring states.

The Persian Wars

At this time Persia had built up a huge **empire** that stretched into **Asia Minor**, and included some Greek settlements. In 499 B.C.E. these cities rebelled against Persian rule and were given help by Athens. This angered Darius, the Persian emperor, and in 490 B.C.E. he sent his army to punish the Greeks. The Athenians defeated the invaders on the plain of Marathon, north of the city.

There was still enormous danger. For the first time in Greek history, over 30 cities throughout the land—notably Athens, Sparta, and Corinth—agreed to join forces to fight the invader. In 480 B.C.E. Darius invaded again with an even bigger force. The Spartans held up the Persian advance with a heroic stand at Thermopylae, and then the combined Greek navy destroyed the enemy fleet at Salamis. The following year the Greek army (led by a Spartan) won a decisive victory at Plataea.

Curved stern ornament, or aplustre

Soldiers defend their ship with spears and stones.

Sailors scramble aboard the ship.

▲ This stone **relief** panel was carved to decorate a tomb in the 100s B.C.E. It illustrates a naval battle between the Greeks and their enemies.

The Peloponnesian Wars

The defeat of the Persians brought great prestige to Athens, helping it to become the leading power in eastern Greece. This was the period when Athens erected magnificent new buildings such as the Parthenon. But as the city grew stronger and richer, its neighbors—especially Sparta—grew jealous, and the long Peloponnesian Wars began.

At first the Athenians refused to fight on land, relying on their strong navy. But then Athens mounted a disastrous expedition to conquer Sicily. The Athenian fleet became trapped inside the harbor at Syracuse, and both fleet and army were wiped out. Athens was permanently weakened. By 404 B.C.E., the great city of Athens was forced to surrender.

Ancient Greece was never a united country. After crushing Athens, Sparta began to bully its allies and even quarreled with the powerful Persians. The chaos continued for another twenty years, until a strong new leader arose out of the remote state of Macedonia.

▼ This map shows major cities and important sites of the ancient Greek world.

King Philip II of Macedonia had a powerful army that subdued the states around him. But just at the height of his success, Philip was murdered. He was succeeded by his twenty-year-old son, Alexander.

Athens' Golden Age

After the Persian Wars, Athens entered its "Golden Age." Under the leadership of Pericles, Athens was made an artistic showplace.

- The temples on the Acropolis, ruined by the Persian attacks, were replaced with a breathtaking group of buildings, including the Parthenon and the Propylaea gateway, shown here. This grand entrance to the Acropolis boasted five elaborate doorways, a blue ceiling covered with gold stars, and a picture gallery.
- Pheidias and other brilliant sculptors carved reliefs and statues, including a giant figure of Athena and Myron's *Discus Thrower*.

Marching to India

Alexander the Great, as he came to be known, turned out to be one of the greatest military leaders in history. He first established complete command in Greece by putting down rebel states. Then he took 37,000 soldiers across the sea to conquer the Persians. One victory followed another, and by 332 B.C.E. Alexander had reached Egypt, where he founded a new city called Alexandria.

Alexander's conquests continued into the east. He marched his army up into the snowy mountains of Afghanistan, down again on to the plains of Pakistan, and across the Indus River into India itself. Finally his exhausted troops rebelled, and in 324 B.C.E. he turned and headed for home. Alexander died the following year, at the age of only 32. He had created a massive **empire**, but there was no new leader strong enough to keep it together, and soon the different regions were fighting each other.

▼ This detail from the Alexander **Mosaic** shows the Persia's King Darius under attack from Alexander, at the Battle of Issus in 333 B.C.E. This mosaic is thought to be a copy made by a Roman artist in the 100s B.C.E. of a Greek-style wall painting that is now lost.

Face of fallen Persian reflected in his shield

King Darius of Persia

Charioteer desperately tries to turn the king's chariot around.

Persian cavalry

Province of Rome

By about 278 B.C.E., the empire had split into three major kingdoms—Egypt, Syria and Babylonia, and Macedonia. Many of the old city-states continued to flourish. This was the start of what is known as the Hellenistic Age (from the word *Hellen,* a name that the Greeks called themselves). It saw the spread of Greek culture through Persia to India and north Africa. In return, new influences transformed Greek art. Palaces were decorated in an oriental (Eastern) manner. Sculpture began to include Egyptian myths and styles, and the Greeks learned to make blown-glass objects.

The Hellenistic Age was ended by the rise of a new and much stronger Mediterranean power—Rome. The Romans defeated Macedonia and destroyed Corinth in 146 B.C.E., making Greece part of their growing empire. The great ages of Greece were over.

▼ The Stoa of Attalus stood in the Agora of Athens. It was originally built by King Attalus in about 140 B.C.E. but was later destroyed by fire. Between 1952 and 1956, the Stoa was carefully reconstructed using some ancient materials.

The spread of Greek culture

Greek ideas, science, language, and religion influenced and changed society in the Near East for more than a thousand years. New Greek cities, such as Alexandria in Egypt, Antioch in Syria, and Pergamum in **Asia Minor**, were magnificently laid out with terraces, colonnades, vast temples, and marketplaces. Sculpture became more ornate and realistic, and featured famous works such as the Winged Victory of Samothrace and the Venus de Milo (the Greek goddess Aphrodite), shown on the left. Elaborate jewelry was produced, as well as molded glass, wall paintings. and mosaics.

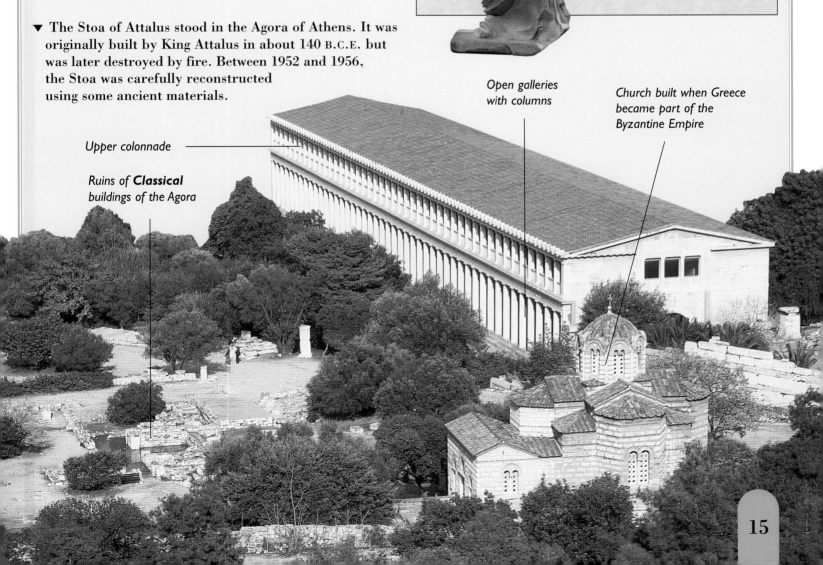

Open galleries with columns

Church built when Greece became part of the Byzantine Empire

Upper colonnade

Ruins of **Classical** buildings of the Agora

Architecture

From about 550 B.C.E., a grand kind of Greek architecture appeared. Previously, buildings had been built of timber, bricks, and plain stones, but now massive temples were built of limestone and marble. There were shrines for the god of each city-state—to Zeus at Olympia, Artemis at Ephesus, and Apollo at Didyma. Other monumental public buildings were theaters, market courts, and assembly halls.

Building a temple

A Greek temple is rectangular, with regular straight sides and square corners. At this time, there was no other way to do it, because no one had learned to build rounded arches or vaults. The roof was made simply by laying beams on top of vertical walls or **columns**. Nevertheless, the Greek style was majestic. Carved columns stood on a stepped stone base. Above them was the horizontal ceiling and above that the pitched roof.

Marble for the temples had to be dug and transported from the quarry, then cut to size and carved by craftspeople using iron tools. The blocks were raised into place and fixed together with **bronze** or iron pins. Finally, the erected stones were decorated, a job that meant polishing the marble, tiling the floor, and **gilding** and coloring statues and paintings.

Who paid for all this? A temple was a public place, so the cost of building was usually met by the taxes levied on the state's citizens, on foreigners, and on **imported** goods. Sometimes wealthy individuals also gave money for these works.

▼ The Athenians built the small Temple of Athena Nike ("victorious") on the Acropolis in 421 B.C.E. to celebrate their defeat of the Persians.

Sculptural frieze showing an assembly of the gods

*Sculptural **frieze** depicting the battle of Marathon*

Fluted columns with Ionic capitals

Temple built from local Pentelic marble

Inner room, or cella, that held a cult statue

Lost Wonder

One of the most amazing of all Greek buildings is no longer standing, but we know about it through the descriptions of Greek and Roman writers, and also through the much later work of **archaeologists**. The Mausoleum at Halicarnassus in **Asia Minor**, built in about 353 B.C.E., was one of the **Seven Wonders of the World**. It was a magnificent tomb, 135 feet (41 meters) high, with three stories—a basement, a colonnade, and then a pyramid. On the very top was a large statue. The Mausoleum was destroyed in an earthquake.

The Parthenon

The temple of the Parthenon is on the highest point of the Acropolis. Work on it began in 447 B.C.E. and took nine years to complete. The temple was dedicated to Athena, goddess of wisdom and warfare, and patron of Athens.

Columns and capitals

Carved columns and horizontal **lintels** are the classic Greek style. Greek columns were not all the same, but had three main styles, or orders. The Doric order

is the simplest, with heavy proportions and little decoration. The Ionic is slimmer, with a ram's horn pattern at the top, or **capital**. The column at left is decorated with two pairs of *volutes* (spiral carved ornaments in the shape of rams' horns). The Corinthian has an even more elaborate capital, decorated with carved leaves.

▼ The Parthenon originally contained a huge ivory and gold statue of the goddess Athena, 39 feet (12 meters) high.

Columns of creamy-white marble, from quarries at nearby Mt Penteli

Inner marble walls, also with a frieze

The roof was once covered in marble tiles.

The pediment, where there were once sculptures showing scenes from **mythology** and Athenian history

A carved frieze stretched for nearly 525 feet (160 meters) around the entire building.

Steps running all around give a rectangular base to the building.

Inside the City-state

Ancient Greece had no capital city. All of the city-states of the Greek world were fiercely independent and frequently fought each other. The stronger ones conquered the weaker ones, taking over their trade and forcing them to provide money and troops for more wars. Several states became very powerful in this way, such as Corinth, Thebes, Samos, and Syracuse in Sicily, but after the Persian Wars two of them—Athens and Sparta—dominated all the others.

Inside Athens

Athens is the most famous example of an ancient **democracy**. The city ruled itself through a government that was elected by its own citizens and bound by its own laws. Citizens were free to give their views at the Assembly, a group that met at least once a week. If a motion they put forward was passed, it became law. Daily running of affairs was in the hands of the Council of 500 citizens, who were chosen by lot once a year. Nobody could serve on the Council for more than two years.

Even so, Athens was not like a modern democracy. A "citizen" had to be male, adult, and Athenian—women, slaves, and foreigners were not allowed to vote or take public office. Nor were citizens always allowed complete freedom of speech. In 399 B.C.E. the great philosopher Socrates was put to death by being forced to drink poison, because things he had said were thought to have undermined the religion and morality of the state.

▼ This marble **relief** carving of Athena, the patron goddess of Athens, was commissioned as a "votive" (religious dedication) for the Acropolis.

Athena was often shown in armor, like this helmet and spear, to illustrate her love of battle.

Athena reads a list of citizens killed in battle, inscribed on this stone.

She wears a peplos, a garment made from a folded rectangle of woolen cloth.

Inside Sparta

Spartan society was organized in a very different way, as a mixture of democracy and monarchy. It had 2 kings, who sat on the state's governing council along with 28 elders chosen by the citizens.

Sparta's main business was war. There was no time to create grand buildings or paint pottery, so comparatively few Spartan works of art have been discovered. Manual work was done by slaves called *helots,* who were mostly inhabitants of a conquered neighbor, Messenia. This left the Spartans free to concentrate on a rigorous system of military training.

Spartan babies were inspected at birth, and the weakest were left to die on an exposed hillside. At the age of seven, the boys were assembled in packs and taught toughness and obedience, playing naked and barefoot. At twenty, they became full soldiers of the state. Girls were encouraged to exercise as fully as the boys, but they did not fight. Their job was to produce more Spartan children.

▼ This **bronze** statue of a boxer, from the first 100 years B.C.E., is a Roman copy of a Greek original. It is slightly bigger than life-size to emphasize the boxer's power.

Weary battle-scarred face with broken nose and battered ears

Bindings on forearms and hands to protect them during a fight

Portraits in stone

Greek sculptors wanted to create beautiful forms, so they showed people looking as perfect as possible, with noble faces. But from about 400 B.C.E., some artists tried to capture the real personality of their subjects. A head of Socrates, for example, depicts a lively, intelligent, but ugly man. An ivory carving of Philip of Macedonia shows that he had lost an eye.

Trade and Warfare

The mountainous landscape of Greece made overland transport very difficult. So it was by sea that Greek settlers explored the Mediterranean. They built up trading links with ports as far apart as southern Spain and north Africa. Trade brought wealth to Greece, and helped spread Hellenic culture.

Traders were looking for goods that were not found in Greece. Some went to Syracuse and southern Italy because of the rich agricultural land. Other sailors bought huge supplies of grain from the shores of the Black Sea. Settlers from the west coast of **Asia Minor** founded Massilia (now Marseilles) in southern France, where they could buy tin and other vital metals.

The port of Piraeus

Attica, the area around Athens, was one of Greece's largest communities from about 450 B.C.E. Its large population—roughly 150,000, plus about 100,000 slaves—needed a huge and regular supply of food, and most of it had to be **imported**. Almost all goods bound for Attica came through the port of Piraeus, a short distance from Athens. Corn, slaves, timber, iron, copper, and luxury items such as scents from Egypt arrived. Meanwhile the locally produced exports—olive oil, wine, pottery, silver, and carvings—were loaded up to be sold abroad. Bankers set up shop in the long colonnades that lined the harbor, ready to buy, sell, or lend money for business ventures.

The fishmonger cuts up a fish on his counter.

Fish head on floor

Comic depiction of a talkative customer

◀ Greek traders and settlers spread around the Mediterranean. This Greek vase was made in southern Italy in the 300s B.C.E.

Soldiers and their weapons

In order to keep hold of these valuable trade routes, the Greeks often had to go to war—against each other and against rival trading nations. We know a lot about the soldiers and their fighting methods because they were frequently pictured on pottery and in sculpture and **relief** carvings. Greeks saw battle as a noble and heroic activity, as well as an ideal subject for art.

The most effective warrior was the hoplite, a heavily armed infantry soldier. His face and head were protected by a plumed **bronze** helmet, and he wore bronze armor on his upper body and legs. Hoplites carried a wooden shield with a bronze rim that prevented splitting, and fought with a long jabbing spear and a short sword. Most armies also had troops of archers and slingers, as well as giant catapults for damaging city walls.

▼ The power of the Greek city-states was often based on their armies. This vase from Corinth in the 600s shows a battle between two hoplite forces.

A helmet covers the ears and most of the face.

Long stabbing spear

Hand grip and arm loop to carry heavy shield

Shield with cockerel emblem, probably a personal motif

Fallen hoplite

Warriors shown nude to indicate their heroic status

Braving the seas

Cargo ships were often clumsy and slow because of their large rounded holds for grain or other goods. They had one big square sail, making them hard to steer. There were no compasses or maps, so ships stayed within sight of land and anchored at night. This vase from the 700s B.C.E., decorated in the Geometric style, shows a Greek warship. You can just make out the lines of rowers and soldiers. The fastest Greek ships were **triremes**—speedy, narrow warships, built with a copper ram in the bow. Powered by 170 rowers who sat in three tiers, a trireme aimed to ram an enemy ship and make a hole below the waterline.

A World of Color

The great sculptor Praxiteles was once asked which of his statues he liked best. He replied, "Those which Nikias painted." We are so used to seeing plain Greek sculptures in museums that it is a surprise to realize that many Greek sculptures were originally colored. Artists used paints, **gilding**, stones, and copper to make the figures look more lifelike. Temples and other buildings were also decorated with bright colors.

We do not see Greek art as the Greeks saw it, when it was part of a living, vibrant **civilization**. We are used to thinking of plain white marble, or dull red **bronze** statues that are usually broken or incomplete in some way. The Venus de Milo has no arms, the Nike of Samothrace has no head, and most warriors have their spears and shields missing. The Greek buildings that remain are at least partly in ruins, and the more important fragments have been taken away to exhibit in museums, with special lighting and spacing.

Originally, of course, all these things were complete, colored in vibrant red, silver, and gold, and made to look as lifelike as possible. They were not simply things to look at, but had a definite purpose. The sculptures and temples were created for the sake of religion and **politics**—not art—and they were not meant to be seen in museums.

The Nike's head has never been found.

Wings held back as the figure lands on board.

Clothing swept back by forward movement

▶ Headless but still magnificent, the Nike (also called the Winged Victory) of Samothrace is depicted landing on the bow of a warship, with swirling clothes to show movement. The sculpture was originally mounted on a fountain to commemorate a sea victory.

Adding color

Artists were coloring their statues as far back as the 500s B.C.E. They rubbed wax paints onto marble carvings to give different shades for hair, eyes, lips, and clothing. Very little of this kind of paint can now be seen, as it has faded or been cleaned away. However, we can get an idea of how vivid the colors were by looking at clay figures and vases from the same period, since their **pigments** are preserved by firing.

Much more original coloring, using metals and stones, has survived on bronze statues. The teeth were inlaid with silver, and the lips and nipples with copper. Eyes were made of stone, either whole pieces or crushed stones made into a paste, and then colored.

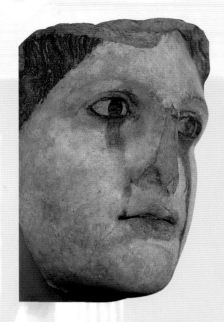

▲ This detail of a marble statue shows how the face was painted.

Three great sculptors

Pheidias (worked c.465 to c.425 B.C.E.) was renowned for his architecture and painting as well as for his sculpture. He was in charge of designing and producing the statues and **relief** decorations for the Parthenon.

Praxiteles (worked c.375 to c.330 B.C.E.) was skilled at conveying the emotion of his subjects in marble. This made him the most famous of Athenian artists. However, hardly any of his work has survived, though several copies by later artists can still be seen. The carved stone head of the goddess Aphrodite shown below is believed to be the work of pupils or followers of Praxiteles.

Lysippus (worked c.340 to c.320 B.C.E.) became the official sculptor for Alexander the Great, who decreed that no one else should be allowed to make his statue. Lysippus was famed for his ability to capture bodies in action. None of his 1,500 bronze figures has survived.

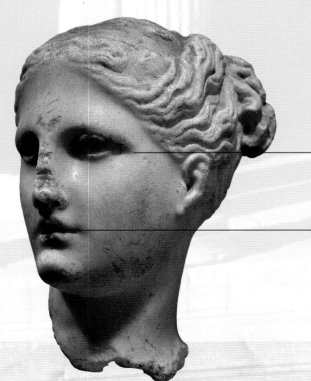

◀ This marble carving of the goddess Aphrodite is from the school of Praxiteles, 325 B.C.E.

Praxiteles was noted for graceful and gently sculpted facial features.

The full mouth is appropriate for Aphrodite, the goddess of love.

Visionaries and Thinkers

The ancient Greeks were among the earliest people to examine the world around them with a view to understanding its nature and the principles that govern it. Early Greek ideas about mathematics and science were far ahead of anything that had been achieved elsewhere in the world, and they underpinned scientific, mathematical, and philosophical progress for many centuries to come.

The power of words

The Greeks had no newspapers or television. There was no printing, so books had to be copied by hand on rolls of **papyrus**. This made them very expensive, and though there were several libraries (notably the one at Alexandria in Egypt, which by about 250 B.C.E. boasted nearly half a million texts), very few people owned a book. The spoken word was therefore very important.

One famous philosopher, Socrates, encouraged others to think about moral questions. He did not preach a specific philosophy but asked questions, hoping that people would realize how ignorant they were. Socrates explored his ideas through discussions but did not write them down.

▲ This sheet of manuscript from the 100s C.E. is part of the only surviving book made of papyrus.

◄ The philosopher Plato is shown talking with his pupils in this Roman **mosaic** from a house in Pompeii—the Italian city was buried by the eruption of the volcano Vesuvius in 79 C.E.

Lessons held outdoors under trees

Plato in dialogue with his pupils

It was Plato, another great philosopher, who wrote down many of Socrates' ideas in the form of "dialogues," or conversations between teacher and pupils.

Herodotus, known as "the Father of History," did not simply record facts like the chroniclers before him. In his massive history of the Persian Wars, he looked at different stories about past events and attempted to explain why they happened.

Epics and lyrics

The first great works of Greek literature started as spoken stories. The **epic** poems *The Iliad* and *The Odyssey*, believed to have been written by Homer at the end of the Dark Ages, were based on tales that had been recited from memory over at least two centuries by skilled storytellers. *The Iliad* narrates episodes from the Trojan Wars, and *The Odyssey* tells of the long journey home of Odysseus, one of the Greeks at Troy. Incidents from the poems were favorite subjects for sculptors and vase painters.

More personal poetry developed all over the Greek world from about 650 B.C.E. Poets wrote about their loves, hates, adventures, and drinking parties, but much of this verse has disappeared. The great female poet Sappho, who lived on the island of Lesbos, is known only through one complete poem and a handful of fragments. On the other hand, the Theban writer Pindar left four entire books of **odes**.

Set in stone

Ancient Greek letters probably developed from the alphabet of the Phoenicians of north Africa, made up of 22 symbols. The earliest Greek texts found by **archaeologists** are scratched on pieces of pottery from about 725 B.C.E. The arrival of writing meant that financial accounts, chronicles, and laws could be recorded on stone tablets.

▶ This inscription from the 100s C.E. shows details of a civic decree about the collection of taxes by city officials. Texts like these give us vital firsthand information about ancient Greece.

Early Greek letters were square, straight figures, suitable for carving with chisel and mallet. Later, many letters became more rounded and simple, as a result of being written in ink.

There were 24 letters in the ancient Greek alphabet, each with its traditional name. The alphabet was adopted by Athens and much of Greece in about 402 B.C.E.

Everyday Life

The warm climate meant that Greeks spent most of their lives outdoors. Houses were not grand and imposing places like the temples and other public buildings. They were usually built around an open courtyard, with a well or covered water tank in the middle. The walls were made of mud bricks baked in the sun, and they had small windows that were covered with wooden shutters to keep out the heat.

Family life went on inside these simple homes. The rooms were not very large, except in rich households. The biggest and fanciest was the dining room, used by the men only. It might have a **mosaic** floor and comfortable couches. There were also workrooms, where the women did the weaving and cooking. The floors here would be plain stone or even beaten earth. Furniture was simple—a few wooden chairs, stools, tables, and storage chests. Many of these items are pictured on vases.

◄ This red-figure pottery painting shows a scene from the interior of a Greek house.

Woman holding **bronze** mirror

High-backed chair with fabric covers

Doorway to a bedroom

A woman's place

The men of the household went out every day to work or to talk with other men in the city. The women spent most of their time indoors and had very little independence. Parents usually arranged marriages, and after women married, they were under their husband's authority. They could not vote or own property. Sparta was the exception, where women lived much freer lives—they were allowed to own property and, although they could not vote, their views were listened to by others.

Housework kept women very busy, although most families had at least one slave to do the hardest jobs. There was cleaning to do, as well as grinding grain and making bread, fetching water, buying provisions, and cooking. Spinning woolen yarn and weaving cloth was important work, making things both to use and to sell.

Greek children

If a baby was born sickly or deformed, it might have a very short life—put into a jar and left out to die in a lonely place. A healthy baby was a cause of great joy in the household. Paintings and clay models show that young children had plenty of toys and games for play—dolls, rattles, spinning tops, and swings. Children also had pets, including hares, tortoises, and dogs. Boys went to school at the age of seven. Schools were private but not expensive. There pupils learned to read, write, and play music and were trained in the basic skills of boxing, wrestling, and athletics. Girls, as always, stayed at home.

The ends of the peplos are pinned at the shoulders.

The waist is fastened with a belt.

To shorten the garment, some of the length is pulled up to hang over the belt.

The rectangle of cloth is wrapped around the wearer under the arms.

Clothes

Most Greeks wore a very simple tunic called a *chiton*, a rectangular piece of linen cloth wrapped around the body and fastened with a brooch or belt. In winter, they also put on a kind of cloak called a *himation*, another square of cloth that was made of wool. On their feet were sandals, though in summer they might go barefoot. The clay figure at right shows a woman wearing a *peplos*.

Vase Painting

We can learn more about ancient Greece from its pottery than almost any other source, partly because there is a lot of it! You might think other art forms would survive better over 2,000 years, but this is not the case. **Bronze** from statues can be melted down and reused, and stone from statues and buildings can be broken up and reused. A broken vase can only be thrown away and left for **archaeologists** to find and put back together. The pictures painted on vases show us a staggering variety of scenes, from athletics, battles, and episodes from **mythology** to simple everyday activities like weaving and winemaking.

▼ This *krater*, or bowl for mixing wine and water, dates from the Geometric period.

Pair of horses depicted almost as one animal, with eight legs and two heads and tails

How vase painting developed

- **Geometric**

  The first great style of decoration began in around 875 B.C.E. It featured geometric shapes, such as straight lines, triangles, and zigzags, painted in bands around the pot. Simple stick figures of humans and animals were painted inside these complex patterns.

- **Black-figure**

  This technique was developed in Corinth in about 720 B.C.E. Painters showed people in much more detail, and began to tell stories in their illustrations. They used black paint for these figures and scratched lines to show details. Later, they also used red and white coloring.

- **Red-figure**

  Around 525 B.C.E., Athenian artists invented a clever new process. Instead of painting black figures, they used the black for the background, and left the figures blank, showing the natural red of the clay. This technique allowed them to add much more delicate detail to the figures, making them more rounded and lifelike.

  Charioteers are carrying round shields with semicircular cutouts on either side.

  Both chariot wheels are shown.

Potters and painters

Clay was one of the most useful and flexible materials in the ancient world. Greeks needed clay pots for everything from storing oil and wine to carrying water and using as prizes. There were potteries in nearly every town or village. Of course, ordinary people used plain, everyday pots, but some pots were beautifully decorated as ornaments or for use in religious ceremonies.

In the 400s B.C.E., Athens became the center for making high-quality painted vases. The craftspeople worked in the Karameikos, or potter's quarter of the city. At this time a few also began to sign their work, either as the maker or the painter—and some did both. Very little is known about these wonderful artists. By careful study, modern scholars can identify the work of some painters, even when there is no signature. These painters are known simply by the place where their works were found or by the subjects painted on them, such as "The Gorgon Painter" and "The Achilles Painter."

The chariot moves towards the viewer.

Red color is used for clothing.

▲ This *krater* from the Attic region shows a chariot drawn by horses, done in the black-figure style.

Using the evidence of pottery

Pottery was made in almost every region of Greece. Each area had its own local styles and shapes. By studying the styles are found in different places, we can develop a picture of how far goods were transported for trade. The age of a pot can also be figured out by examining how it was decorated.

◀ This Attic cup from about 490 B.C.E. is done in the red-figure style. The image shows a scene from Homer's *Iliad*, with the slave girl Briseis and Phoenix, friend of Achilles.

Playing Games

Many Greeks were rich enough to employ slaves to do most of the work, so they had plenty of spare time, and they spent some of it playing games. Greek artists have left images of several of these activities, including ball games, board games, knucklebones, and an unusual game called kottabos that involved flicking the drops of a glass of wine at a target. Although kottabos was played by men at parties, other games were enjoyed by adults and children alike.

Knucklebones is shown on several vases and sculptures. It was popular because all it required were five ankle bones from small, cloven-footed animals. The game involved throwing and catching the bones in various different ways, like the modern game of jacks. For example, the player could throw up the first bone, pick up another while it was in the air, and then catch the first bone as it came down. A second stage was played by throwing two bones up in the air while picking up a third, and so on.

Children's games

Games with hoops and tops were popular among young children. They played ball games, including one with a stick and ball that looks similar to hockey. Paintings also show a game of piggyback, in which a blindfolded child has to find her way to a set point while carrying one of her friends.

▼ A game of knucklebones is played by the two girls in this sculpture. It is not clear from the statuette which stage the game has reached—they may be about to place the bones on the ground, ready to play.

This statuette is made of terra cotta, a reddish unglazed mix of clay and sand. The girl holds one bone in her right hand. Is she about to throw it, or place it on the ground?

The girl holds two knucklebones in her left hand.

Board games

The ancient Greeks played board games, but we do not know much about them. One writer describes a game called "five lines," a kind of tic-tac-toe played on a board with counters. One of the best pieces of artistic evidence for board-game playing is a vase painting (right) by Exekias, a famous Athenian artist from the 500s B.C.E. for his black-figure vase decoration. It shows the heroes Achilles and Ajax playing a board game. The two men are in armor, and they are presumably playing during a quiet period in the Trojan Wars.

Vase painters portrayed their subjects from the side, in profile. This means that this vase provides good evidence of the two heroes' clothes and armor, but it is impossible to see the board. In spite of this, the painting does give us some information. No tall playing pieces can be seen, so the game is probably played with flat counters. Both men are reaching for the board at the same time. So the game is likely to be played quickly, unlike elaborate strategy games such as chess.

Games in Athens and Sparta

Athens and Sparta had different attitudes about game playing. In Athens there are many pictures showing people taking part in sports, but there is also plenty of evidence that the Athenians enjoyed pastimes like board games and knucklebones. The Spartans, however, emphasized fitness above all and chose sports like running and wrestling rather than board games. In Sparta, girls as well as boys took part in these sports, but when Athenian artists showed girls relaxing, they were usually playing games like knucklebones.

Both figures hold their spears, suggesting that this is a quick game played during a lull in fighting.

Ajax leans forward to move a counter.

Flat playing surface

▲ The two heroes Achilles and Ajax play a board game on this vase, painted in the black-figure style. The vase is a rounded type that **archaeologists** call a "belly amphora." It was used for the storage of grain, oil, or wine.

Eating and Drinking

The warm, dry climate of Greece made it easy to grow some crops. Greek farmers produced barley and wheat as well as olives, figs, and nuts. They dug up the soil with plows drawn by oxen, or used spades and hoes if they had no animals. However, most of Greece is mountainous and has little flat and fertile land. Flocks of sheep and goats could be grazed here, but little could be grown. As their populations increased, many city-states had to **import** vital stocks of grain from settlements in Italy and near the Black Sea.

Rich and poor

The Greeks ate little during the day. A snack of olives or fruit at sunrise might be followed by a light lunch at midday, or nothing at all. The main meal was eaten at sunset after the day's work was done. For poor people, this usually meant beans or barley that had been soaked and made into soup or a kind of paste that was mixed with spices and baked. The lucky ones had plenty of olives, cheese, and fruit to eat, while many kept hens to provide them with eggs.

Only richer people could afford to buy fish or meat regularly, and this was usually roasted on a spit over an open fire. The rich also ate bread made from wheat flour, a finer and more expensive flour than that made from barley. There was no sugar, so food was sweetened with honey, a sweetener that became an important crop. The honeybee colonies were kept in hives made of wood, reeds, or even clay.

▼ This black-figure vase, made in Athens in about 520 B.C.E., shows a scene from country life.

Climbing into the tree to reach the high branches

One farmer picks up the fallen olives.

Farmers use sticks to knock down olives from the tree.

Hunting and fishing

In ancient times, woodland still covered much of the hills and mountains. There were many wild animals, such as boar and deer, and hunting them was a good way of putting meat in the cooking pot. Greeks hunted on foot with spears and bows, though they also caught game in snares and nets. We know this from many illustrations on **mosaics** and painted pottery.

The sea was an even more important source of tasty food. Many fishing boats worked along Greece's long coastline, bringing in a great variety of fish including tuna, red mullet, octopus, and anchovies. These were sold fresh or pickled in salt to keep them through the winter. Poor people made their soup taste more exciting by putting in small amounts of salted fish.

▶ The painting on this plate shows a hunter returning home with his dog, carrying the rabbits he has caught.

A dinner party

A Greek dinner party was called a *symposium*, which means "drinking together." We know a lot about these events from many written descriptions, and from painted vases, such as this red-figure-style painting from an amphora. The men ate and drank while lying on couches. The wine was mixed with water in a special large vessel called a *krater* and then served out by slaves.

All wear woolen bands around their heads.   *A slave brings wine.*

A woman entertains the group with music.

Dish of snacks

The men recline on elaborate couches with plenty of cushions.

Theater and the Olympic Games

Some of the most spectacular buildings that remain from ancient Greece are the theaters—vast auditoriums such as the 14,000-seat theater at Epidaurus. At Delphi there are remains of the Olympic stadium, a building that seated 7,000 spectators.

The ancient Greeks invented the theater and the Olympic Games, but unlike plays and sports today, these events were not held simply to amuse people. They were usually part of much bigger religious festivals, organized to please the gods and to bring peace and prosperity. Each city had its own festivals throughout the year, when the whole population took a holiday to enjoy the excitement of the occasion.

Greek drama

Greek theater probably started in about 550 B.C.E. in the songs and dances performed in honor of Dionysus, the god of wine. In Athens this practice developed into a four-day drama festival called the Dionysia, with processions and **sacrifices** followed by as many as five different plays each day. Athens of the 400s B.C.E. produced some of the greatest playwrights of all time, including Aeschylus and Sophocles (who wrote tragedies) and Aristophanes (who wrote comedies). Some of their work is still performed today.

All the people on stage were men, who wore masks over their faces. Most of them formed the **chorus**, who commented on events in the play but did not take part in the action. Scenery and costumes were often lavish, and prizes were given to the best writers, producers, and actors.

▼ This marble bust of the playwright Sophocles is a Roman copy of a Greek work from the 300s B.C.E., now lost.

Jagged edge of marble probably copies the broken Greek original.

Plinth, or base of statue

The Olympic Games

Many religious festivals involved athletic competitions. The biggest and most famous of these were the Olympic Games, first held in 776 B.C.E. at Olympia in honor of Zeus, father of the gods, who was believed to live on Mount Olympus. Weeks beforehand, heralds throughout Greece announced the games, and warring states called a truce so that people could travel safely.

The five-day games began with sacrifices to Zeus and other ceremonies, and then the competition got under way with a race between chariots pulled by four horses. Then came more horse races and the pentathlon, combination of wrestling, long jump, discus, javelin, and 200-meter race. There were boxing and pankration (all-out fighting) contests, as well as long-distance running races and even a race in which the competitors wore armor. Only the winner received a prize—a wreath of olive leaves.

A runner practices his starting position.

Each wrestler tries to get a firm grip on his opponent's arms, ready to throw him.

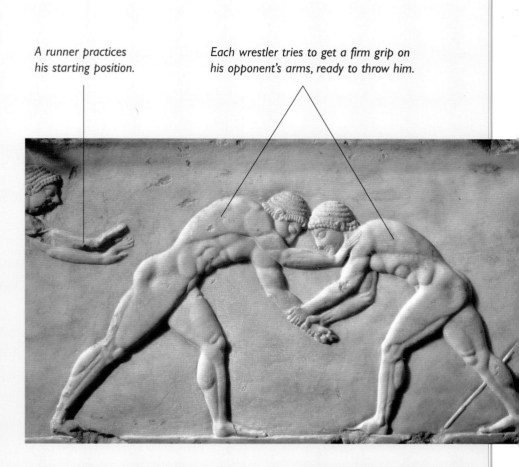

▲ This marble **relief** carving of athletes wrestling was originally produced to adorn an Athenian statue's base in about 510 B.C.E.

A night at the theater

Nearly every Greek city had a theater. One of the most famous was at Epidaurus. It was a huge open-air structure with 54 tiers of seats set into a semicircle in the hillside. It was so perfectly built that an actor speaking in a normal voice could be heard on the very top tier. The theater's stone seats were hollowed out below so people could tuck their legs in). People probably brought cushions to sit on and food and wine to keep them going during the performance, since it lasted several hours. The vast bowl of the theater of Epidaurus was originally built as part of a sanctuary dedicated to Asclepius, the god of healing.

Religion and Mythology

Religion occupied a central place in the lives of the ancient Greeks. They believed that the gods controlled all aspects of their lives. If these gods became angry, they would send disaster and bad luck. So the Greeks worked hard to please them, with prayers and **sacrifices**, elaborate festivals, and grand temples.

The gods might be frightening, but they were not beasts or monsters. The Greeks saw them as looking just like humans, sometimes moving among ordinary people and taking part in their daily lives. They had the same feelings and faults, although they never grew old or lost their strength. Much of what we know about Greek **mythology** comes from statues. Sculptors and painters showed the gods and goddesses as ideal beings, perfect and beautiful. The many stories about them form the basis of Greek myths.

The family of gods

There were a bewildering number of gods, but the twelve most important ones lived on Mount Olympus, the highest mountain in Greece.

Zeus, the king of the gods, was the most powerful of the gods and ruled the skies, sending fine weather or storms. When he was angry, he would hurl his deadly thunderbolts.

Hera, Zeus's wife, was the goddess of children and marriage.

Poseidon, Zeus's brother, was god of the sea. He drove a chariot through the waters, drawn by foaming white horses, and his weapon was a trident.

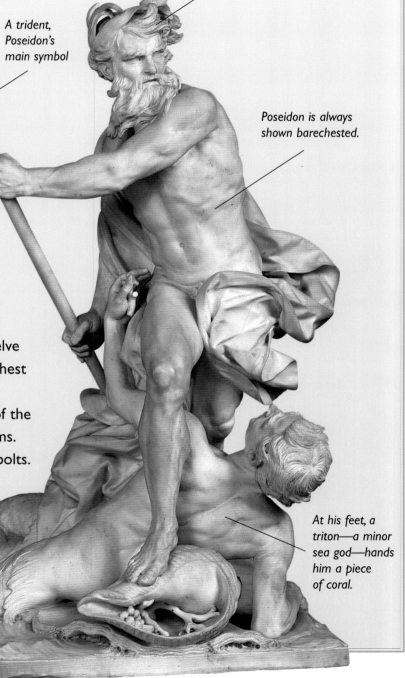

▼ The Greek gods have inspired countless artists since **Classical** times. This marble statue of Poseidon was carved by Lambert-Sigisbert Adam in 1757.

Thick beard and wild hair

A trident, Poseidon's main symbol

Poseidon is always shown barechested.

At his feet, a triton—a minor sea god—hands him a piece of coral.

▲ This vast ceiling painting of the gods on a cloudy Mount Olympus was completed in 1528 by the Italian artist Giulio Romano and his assistants.

Demeter was the goddess of farming and crops. When her daughter was kidnapped by Hades, she made the earth barren until the girl was released and then restored fertility. This explained the different seasons of the year.

Hestia was goddess of the home and hearth. Many Greeks kept a fire burning in her honor.

Athena, a daughter of Zeus, was goddess of wisdom and warfare, arts and crafts, and patron goddess of Athens.

Apollo was god of light and music. The best loved of all the gods, he also was also associated with archery, medicine, and prophecy—telling the future.

Artemis was goddess of the moon and hunting. Twin sister of Apollo, she spent her time in the woods of Arcadia, hunting wild animals with her hounds.

Hermes was the messenger of the gods. He conducted dead people to the Underworld. Hermes was also a trickster who loved to tell lies and could make himself invisible.

Aphrodite was goddess of beauty and love. One of Zeus's many daughters, she was born out of the foam that the sea washed up on the shore.

Hephaestus was god of metal crafts and fire, who knew how to make many magical objects, including a gold watchdog for Zeus.

Ares was god of war. He was not popular with the other gods, because he represented the rage and violence of warfare.

▶ The black-figure painting on this amphora shows the goddess Demeter, Persephone, and Triptolemus.

Triptolemus, teacher of the skills of agriculture, on his magical wheeled throne

The goddess Demeter and Persephone, her daughter

Festivals and Oracles

The aim of Greek religion was to please the gods. This meant **sacrifices** and festivals and elaborate ceremonies, to make the gods happy and friendly towards the mortals. If the correct **rituals** were performed, the gods would send large harvests, victory in war, or other good things. If the gods were neglected, they might send storms, defeat, and all kinds of disasters.

People made sure that the gods also looked after their homes and families. Outside the front door they kept a small statue of Hermes to guard against burglary, while inside a fire burned in the hearth to honor Hestia. In the courtyard there was usually an altar to Zeus as protector and defender of the household.

Public religion

Every city and village had its calendar of religious festivals. In Athens there were more than 60 events throughout the year. These ranged from huge ceremonies, with games, dancing, and even beauty contests, to much smaller celebrations for a local god within a tribe or family. Greeks looked forward to these events as holidays and as times to enjoy themselves together.

▲ The sanctuary of Apollo at Delphi was thought to be the center of the world. It was marked by this mysterious *omphalos* stone, shaped like a navel or an egg, that stood outside the temple. The marble is carved with wreaths.

The biggest festivals, celebrating the major gods, were for people from all over the Greek world. Zeus was honored at the games at Olympia and Nemeaa—where the victors won crowns of celery. The Pythian Games at Delphi were dedicated to Apollo and included musical competitions. The Isthmian Games at Corinth were in honor of Poseidon. All of these meetings featured **sacrifices** and solemn prayers.

◄ A musical competition depicted on a vase made in about 510 B.C.E.

Judges carry staves to show their official function.

A performer mounts the stage.

The work of a priest

The council of the city-state elected the priests for a city's temples—usually men for the male gods and women for the female ones. The priests conducted the religious **rituals** and were expected to know proper words and actions for the ceremonies. On top of this, they were responsible for the upkeep of the buildings, whitewashing the walls, and making repairs.

Another important religious figure was the prophet or seer. This person had to explain the meaning of omens and how they showed what would happen in the future. An omen could be anything from a dream to the flight of a bird, but only prophets could correctly interpret what it meant. Some of them told the future by inspecting the insides of sacrificial animals.

Consulting the oracle

In special circumstances, the gods would answer questions about the future asked by worshipers. This could be done at sacred sites called **oracles**. There were several oracles throughout Greece, including the famous sanctuary of Apollo at Delphi. At the Dodona oracle in Epirus, people wrote their questions on lead tablets, and received the answers in the sound of the wind in a sacred oak tree.

▼ This picture shows the *tholos* at the sanctuary of Athena at ancient Delphi. This graceful circular monument once had twenty Doric **columns**. Nobody knows exactly how it was used.

Bases of outer ring of columns

Three columns reerected in 1938

Circular platform of tholos *building*

Heroes and Heroines

Greeks loved and honored their heroes almost as much as their gods. These heroes may once have been real people, but they had been turned into legends as demigods, or beings halfway between humans and gods. The Greeks believed that they had been born as ordinary mortals, but became godlike because they performed great deeds of strength or courage. However, in the end they would die and go to the Underworld.

Tales about heroes and heroines were passed down by storytellers. Many of them became cult figures, who were worshiped with special ceremonies at local shrines. The Greeks saw heroes as examples to copy and also as people who might help them communicate with the true gods. All the same, not all heroes were completely heroic. There were many imperfect and vulnerable characters who acted in ways that were very human.

Herakles

The most famous of all the mythical heroes, even today, is Herakles or Hercules. The original Herakles was possibly a leader in Mycenaean times, but over the centuries he was turned into a hero. People believed he was the son of Zeus and a mortal woman. He was enormously strong. The story goes that when he was just a baby in his cradle, he strangled two snakes sent to kill him.

Herakles is best known for the twelve labors (tasks) he had to complete. These amazing deeds included killing the Nemean lion with his bare hands, destroying the human-eating Stymphalian birds, and capturing the three-headed guard dog of the underworld.

▶ For his second labor, Herakles had to kill the poisonous water snake called the Hydra. It kept growing new heads whenever he chopped one off. The **Renaissance** artist Giambologna created this **bronze** in the 1500s C.E.

Sculpture shows a club, though in legend Herakles killed the Hydra with his sword.

One of the Hydra's nine heads

Clawed serpent's feet

Theseus and the Minotaur

Theseus was the national hero of Athens and the son of either Aegeus, the king of Athens, or the god Poseidon. He had many adventures showing his daring and strength, though he is best remembered for his voyage to Crete. His mission was to find and kill the Minotaur, a monster that was half human and half bull and lived in an underground maze called the Labyrinth. Theseus was helped by Ariadne, a Cretan princess, who gave him a ball of thread that he unwound as he made his way into the Labyrinth. Having slain the Minotaur, he found his way out again by following the thread. He sailed away with Ariadne, though he later abandoned her, and became king of Athens.

Monsters of myth

Artists loved to depict the many weird beasts that appear in the Greek myths. Many of them are mixtures of more than one animal. Medusa the Gorgon was a mortal woman, whose hair was made of writhing snakes and whose face was so horrible that anyone who saw it was turned to stone. The Hydra had the body of a dog and nine snake-like heads which grew back double when chopped off. The fire-breathing Chimera had the head of a lion, the body of a goat and the tail of a snake. This black-figure vase from the 500s B.C.E. shows Theseus fighting the Minotaur in the Labyrinth.

Theseus wrestles with the monster.

Ariadne watches the fight.

Minotaur with bull's head

Marble and Bronze

reek sculptors had several materials to choose from. The earliest carvers probably made statues of wood, but these have rotted and none has been found. Some used clay, but this broke easily and was only suitable for small pieces. Stone and **bronze** statues were stronger and lasted far longer, even though they were much more expensive and time consuming to produce.

The main purpose of Greek sculpture was religious. City governments or rich citizens paid for the works that were put on display in sanctuaries and temples and dedicated to the gods. One of the greatest of all these statues, the massive bronze figure of Athena designed by Pheidias, was put up to thank the goddess for the Greek victory over the Persians. Pheidias and other skilled sculptors could ask high fees for such work, and became celebrities.

▶ The *Discus Thrower* is a celebrated portrayal of motion frozen in stillness. This is a marble copy by a Roman artist of the lost **bronze** sculpture created by Myron in about 450 B.C.E. The original was so highly praised by **Classical** writers that it was copied many times for wealthy Roman buyers.

The thrower is caught at the moment between his backswing and his foreswing.

The discus thrower turns his body as he prepares to launch the discus. Greek sculpture conveys power and emotion, in contrast to the stiff poses of Egyptian art.

The tree stump is there to support the heavy marble. It spoils the purity of the statue, and would not have been in Myron's original (lighter) bronze.

Carving stone

A sculptor could take as long as a year to complete a life-size marble statue. He would work in his workshop or travel to where the sculpture was needed. Besides his wages, there was also the cost of quarrying and transporting the block of marble. With all this expense, sculptors had to take great care. Even marble can crack and splinter, so there was no room for mistakes.

First, the artist marked the marble block with a grid of lines. Then, an outline was sketched of the desired figure—front, back, and sides—on top of this. The grid allowed the artist to make the proportions match on all four sides. Using a mallet and a rough pointed chisel, the artist chipped away the excess stone. Once this work had been done, finer tools could be used and then special powders applied to finish and smooth off the statue.

Casting bronze

To produce a bronze statue, the sculptor had to begin by making a clay model, sometimes built up on a wooden center. The sculptor covered this with a thin coating of wax and placed it inside a mold that was also made of clay. The whole thing was then heated, so that the clay baked hard and the wax melted and ran out. This left a narrow gap between mold and model. Molten bronze was poured in to fill the space, and when it cooled the mold was taken away. The sculptor could now fill in holes or file away rough edges.

Bronze statues were hollow. This made them much lighter than stone. Sculptors were able to make far more delicate pieces, because the thinner parts (such as legs and arms) did not have to support the weight of marble. They could also put weights inside the hollow sections to balance the statue so that it retained its pose.

▼ Bronze head of an unknown god or hero, from the 100s B.C.E.

Blank holes for eyes were probably filled with decorative stone.

Hollow inside where the original clay model was

Time line

(All dates B.C.E.)

Early history and the Dark Ages (dates approximate)

1600–1200
Mycenaean **civilization** is at its height.

1450
Mycenaeans build palaces at Tiryns, Thebes, Pylos, and elsewhere.

1220
possible date of the Trojan Wars between Greeks and Troy

1200–1150
Mycenaean sites are destroyed.

1100–1000
Dorian people invade Greece.

1050
beginning of Greek migration to islands and **Asia Minor**.

Rise of the city-states

875
Geometric pottery begins to be made.

776
First Olympic Games are held.

750–700
possible dates for writing of Homer's *Iliad* and *Odyssey*

733
Corinth founds Syracuse in Sicily.

730
Sparta begins conquest of Messenia.

720
development of black-figure vase painting

c.700
First Doric temples built.

683
First *archon* (nonroyal leader) appointed in Athens.

Archaic Age

c.650–510
Tyrants rule in Corinth, Miletus, Athens, Samos, and other cities.

630
First known male nude marble statues are made.

621
Draco writes Athens' first code of laws.

600
Temple of Hera is built at Olympia.

c.590
Sappho writing poetry on Lesbos

c.585
First Pythian Games are held at Delphi.

546
Persians take control of Ionia.

530
Pythagoras, philosopher and mathematician, is active in southern Italy.

525
development of red-figure vase painting

498
Pindar is writing poetry in Thebes.

490
First Persian invasion of Greek mainland; Greek victory at Marathon.

480
Second Persian invasion; Battle of Thermopylae; sack of Athens; and Greek victory at Salamis.

479
Greeks defeat Persians at Plataea.

Classical Age

478
Delian League is formed by Greek cities against Persia.

c.470
Temple of Zeus at Olympia is built.

470–425
careers of sculptors Pheidias and Polyclitus, and playwrights Euripides, Sophocles, and Aeschylus

461–445
first Peloponnesian War between Athens and Sparta

454
Delian League treasury moves to Athens.

447
Building of Parthenon begins in Athens.

438
Statue of Athena is made for the Parthenon.

431–404
Second Peloponnesian War

431
Thucydides begins writing his histories.

430
Statue of Zeus is erected at Olympia.

c.430
beginning of Aristophanes' career

429
death of Pericles

420
Temple of Apollo at Bassae is built.

415–413
Athenian expedition to Syracuse

404
Athens surrenders to Sparta.

401
Greek expedition to Persia

399
death of Socrates

396
beginning of the career of Plato

395–386
war of Sparta against Corinth, Thebes, and Argos, plus the Persians

371
Thebes defeats Sparta at Leuctra.

Alexander and the Hellenistic Age

359
Philip II becomes king of Macedonia.

358
Theater at Epidaurus is built.

356
Alexander the Great is born.

353
Mausoleum at Halicarnassus is built.

338
Philip defeats Athens and Thebes at Chaeronea.

336
death of Philip II

335
Aristotle begins teaching in Athens.

334
Alexander leads army into Persia.

332
Alexander conquers Egypt and founds Alexandria.

326
Alexander reaches the Indus River.

323
death of Alexander

295
Library is founded at Alexandria.

279
Greece is invaded by Gaul.

146
sack of Corinth; Greece becomes part of Roman **Empire**

Glossary

archaeologist person who finds, studies, and preserves the remains of ancient civilizations

aristocrat member of a class of nobles who ruled in Greece for a period of time

artifact object made by people, such as a tool or weapon

Asia Minor southwestern part of Asia (much of modern Turkey)

bronze alloy (mixture) of copper and tin, and sometimes other metals

capital topmost, decorated section of a column

cast form metal into a shape by pouring hot, liquid metal into a mold

chorus in Greek drama, a group of people who speak together, usually commenting on the action of the play

civilization system of social development

classical having to do with the ancient Greeks and Romans, especially their art, architecture, and literature

column pillar supporting part of a building or standing alone as a monument

democracy rule by the people through elected representatives

empire group of countries under the rule of one state

epic long poem telling the story of one or more heroes

frieze horizontal band of sculpture along the upper part of a wall

gild cover with a thin layer of gold

immigrant someone who enters another country to settle there

import bring in goods from another country

lintel horizontal beam of wood or stone over a door or window

mosaic picture or design formed with tiny pieces of colored stone, tile, or glass

mythology body of myths, or traditional stories dealing with supernatural beings and happenings, often made up as a way of explaining a country's origins, history, and religion

ode poem meant to be sung by a chorus at a Greek play

oracle shrine where ancient Greeks went to ask their gods to give advice or to foretell the future

papyrus early form of paper made from the pressed and woven stems of the papyrus reed

pigment substance that gives something color, such as paint or dye

politics art or science of government

relief method of carving or sculpture in which pictures are raised to stand out from the background

Renaissance period at the end of the Middle Ages, around the 1400s C.E., marked by a revival of interest in the arts and learning of ancient Greece and Rome

ritual special wordds and actions used to perform a cereemony, often religious in nature

sacrifice offering given to please or honor a god, often involving the ritual killing of an animal

Seven Wonders of the World seven amazing structures from the ancient world: the pyramids of Egypt, the hanging gardens of Babylon, the temple of Artemis at Ephesus, the statue of Zeus at Olympia, the Mausoleum at Halicarnassus, the Colossus of Rhodes and the Pharos (lighthouse) at Alexandria

trireme Greek warship powered by oars set in three tiers

Further Resources

Books

Bardi, Pieri. *The Atlas of the Classical World*. New York: McGraw-Hill, 2001.

Belloli, Andrea. *Exploring World Art*. Los Angeles: Getty Publications, 1999.

Day, Nancy. *Your Travel Guide to Ancient Greece*. Minneapolis, Minn.: Lerner Publishing, 2000.

Greenblatt, Miriam. *Alexander the Great and Ancient Greece*. Tarrytown, N.Y.: Marshall Cavendish, 1999.

Hammond, Paula. *Cultures and Costumes: Greece and Turkey*. Broomall, Penn.: Mason Crest, 2002.

Hull, Robert. *The World of Ancient Greece: Everyday Life*. Danbury, Conn.: Scholastic Library, 2000.

Hull, Robert. *The World of Ancient Greece: Religion and the Gods*. Danbury, Conn.: Scholastic Library, 2000.

Hull, Robert. *The World of Ancient Greece: Trade and Warfare*. Danbury, Conn.: Scholastic Library, 2000.

Jovinelly, Joann, and Jason Netelkos. *The Crafts and Culture of the Ancient Greeks*. New York: Rosen Publishing, 2001.

Knight, Judson. *Ancient Civilizations*. Farmington Hills, Mich.: Gale Group, 2000.

Malam, John. *Greek Town*. Danbury, Conn.: Scholastic Library, 2000.

Miles, Lisa. *Encyclopedia of Ancient Greece*. Tulsa, Okla.: EDC Publishing, 2000.

Pearson, Anne. *Ancient Greece*. New York: Dorling Kindersley, 2000.

Powell, Anton, and Sean Sheehan. *Ancient Greece*. New York: Facts on File, 2003.

Woods, Mary B., and Michael Woods. *Ancient Construction*. Minneapolis, Minn.: Lerner, 2000.

Index

Achilles 9, 31
Acropolis 4, 13, 16, 17
Ajax 9, 31
Alexander the Great 13, 14, 23
Alexandria 14, 15, 24
alphabet 25
Aphrodite 15, 23, 37
Apollo 16, 37, 38, 39
architecture 4, 7, 16–17
Athena 7, 17, 18, 37, 39
Athena Nike 16
Athens 4, 5, 7, 12–13, 15, 17, 18, 23, 28, 29, 31, 34, 38, 41

children 19, 27, 30, 31
Chimera 41
city-states 10–11, 18–19
clothes 27
Corinth 10–11, 12, 15, 18, 28, 38

Darius, emperor of Persia 12, 14
Delphi 7, 34, 38, 39

Egypt 9, 11, 14, 15, 20
Ephesus 7, 16
Epidaurus 5, 34, 35

family life 26–27
festivals 34–35, 36, 38
food 20, 32–33

gods 9, 34, 35, 36–37, 38, 39

Hephaestus 37
Herakles 40

Hermes 37, 38
Hestia 37, 38
Homer 9, 25, 29

India 14, 15
Issus, battle of 14

Knossos 7

Lion Gate, Mycenae 8

Macedonia 13, 15
mathematics 24
Mausoleum at Halicarnassus 17
Medusa 41
Messenia 19
Minotaur 41
mosaics 14, 15, 24, 26
Mycenae 8, 9
mythology 5, 7, 9, 36–37, 40–41

Nike 5, 22

Odysseus 9
Olympia 16, 35, 38
Olympic Games 34–35
omphalos stone 38

Panathenaic Festival 7
Parthenon 4, 5, 6, 7, 13, 17, 23
Peloponnesian Wars 13
Persian War 12, 25, 42
Philip II, king of Macedonia 13, 19
philosophy 24–25
Piraeus 20

Plato 24, 25
poetry 25
Poseidon 36, 38, 41
pottery 4, 5, 11, 28, 29
Propylaia 13

Rome 15

science 24
sculptors 5, 6, 13, 19, 22, 23, 42–43
sculpture 4, 15, 19, 22–23, 42–43
Seven Wonders of the World 17
Socrates 18, 19, 24, 25
soldiers 9, 14, 19, 21
Sparta 12–13, 18, 19, 27, 31
Stoa of Attalus, Athens 15
Syracuse 13, 18, 20

temples 4, 6, 11, 13, 15, 16, 22, 36, 39, 42
theater 5, 34, 35
Thebes 7, 18
Theseus 41
trade 11, 12, 18, 20–21, 29
Trojan Wars 9, 25

vase painting 7, 9, 11, 28–29, 31, 32
Venus de Milo 15, 22

Winged Victory of Samothrace 15, 22
women 18, 26–27, 33, 39

Zeus 7, 16, 35, 36, 37, 38